SPANS

SPANS

new and selected poems

ELIZABETH SEYDEL MORGAN

Louisiana State University Press)I(*Baton Rouge*

Published by Louisiana State University Press
Copyright © 2014 by Elizabeth Seydel Morgan
All rights reserved
Manufactured in the United States of America
LSU Paperback Original
First printing

Designer: Barbara Neely Bourgoyne
Typeface: Utopia

The author wishes to thank the editors of the journals and periodicals in which some of these poems appeared: *Blackbird:* "A D D" and "Widow's Walk"; *Connotation Press:* "August Evening" and February Burglary"; *Poetry:* "September 2011" and "The Span"; *The Raleigh New and Observer:* "A Poem Too Short For Its Subject."

Library of Congress Cataloging-in-Publication Data
Morgan, Elizabeth Seydel, 1939–
  [Poems. Selections]
  Spans : new and selected poems / Elizabeth Seydel Morgan.
    pages ; cm
  ISBN 978-0-8071-5706-0 (pbk. : alk. paper) — ISBN 978-0-8071-5707-7 (pdf) —
ISBN 978-0-8071-5708-4 (epub) — ISBN 978-0-8071-5709-1 (mobi)
  I. Title.
  PS3563.O828A6 2014
  811'.54—dc23

                                                                              2014001663

to Cameron, Jack, Hope, Anna and Matthew

Contents

ON LONG MOUNTAIN

WITHOUT A PHILOSOPHY

NEW POEMS

PARTIES

The Party before the Party

Late sun changed the bottles
to stained-glass colors
on the white tablecloth
that covered the bar.

Little girls in pinafores
played tag and touch
under old locusts and Japanese Maples.
They fluttered like the pattern
of shadows the breeze and the star
leaves made on the lawn.

Laughter was light, light
was light, iced drinks were light
at the party before the party.

We were lovely as children,
lingering maturely, but itchy
as children, hardly bearing
to stand so still,
ready to run and hide and seek.

I was a grownup, wearing a sundress
that left my back bare. You
came up beside me and lightly,
but with your whole hand,
touched me there.

Every Fact Is a Field

> In the language of science, every fact is a field.
> —Jacob Bronowski

It is summer on your father's farm,
South Georgia, 1956.
We are teenaged girls.

Our bare legs straddle the bare backs
of palomino quarter horses
who're nuzzling and munching clover,
the reins loose on their golden necks.

The clover is blooming, a purple field
sloping away from this knoll
to a dark stand of pines
that hides half the sun.

We're sharing a stolen cigarette,
feeling horsewarmth against our thighs,
the June air cooling on our moist skin.

We talk so long the sky draws up
the clover's color to its own field.

The horses snort, then shift.
Your leg touches mine as we watch in silence
the black pines rise,
pulling this land up and over,
taking us backward into night.

Without a word we rein our horses
and turn their heads, mine left, yours right.

That evening is a fact.
I am still here in its field.

The Party

It's an old story, what happens later.
How dark the dance is, how loud, how drunk.
Talking is shouting, touching a joke.
Shadows of solo dancers writhe like snakes
up the walls of the barn to the rafters
and sink down again when the music breaks,
and rise and fall, and rise and fall in the smoke.

The Adamsons' Peacocks

Brakes screech, heavy metal thunks. A second, then glass crashes.
Behind my woods there's been another wreck on Three Chopt Road.

Waiting for the sirens makes me hear the silence,
And in that silence come uncanny human cries for help.

I've lived here long enough to know this cry
Is like, but only like, a woman's in the labor room,

Or a woman slammed against a wall with two hands on her shoulders
Who knows that what those hands do next will kill her in some way.

Help, oh, help, oh, help: the desperate aspirants of pain,
The long vowels of howling the long hours of the first birth.

Or the cry you tried to stifle, trying to be quiet, to hide
From someone—the parents, the children—the truest sound you make.

The way a peacock calls its mate: unseemly, raucous, screamed.
Like brakes too late, like any passion over the limit,

Beyond the gorgeous plumage, after the measured dancing,
Past any sequential ritual we ever learned.

Counting Sheep

The drunk in the kitchen is Mother.
The dry metal *crack* is the ice tray.
The long liquid silence is whiskey.
The spigot's quick gush is the water.
The cupboard doors banging is searching.
The one-sided talking is pleading.
The God-damning sobbing is praying.
The dry metal *crack* is the ice tray.
The drunk in the kitchen is Mother.

Heron

The moment between what wasn't
and what is
has to shock like the instant
I saw the three-foot heron
perched like a prank
in my front yard.

I've known a few annunciations.
My God I'm in love was one,
and the bloodied baby's head
between my thighs. Then
my thin son with a suitcase,
losing resolution
in my rearview mirror.

The elegant heron stood in my yard,
in my cluttered neighborhood,
miles from water, fish, its kind.
It curled and uncurled its neck,
scanning the air for bearings.

All morning I thought
it would fly away.
By afternoon I was afraid
it never would.

Who could miss this incongruous sight?
Everyone who passed by did.
Walkers, drivers, runners, children
never noticed the Great Blue Heron
dying by my Pontiac.

It stood there all day long,
bearing its weight
on legs as frail as marsh grass.

Halloween

I. Stuart Circle Hospital

They gave me no choice, dried
my milk with a shot, tried
to make me sleep.

But I lie here and watch the light fall
through gingko and maple, the last
of the fans and the golden stars
brushing Jeb Stuart, settling
on the brim of his bronze plumed hat.

On this last afternoon in October
the piles of leaves on Stuart Circle
are high enough to hide a child,
and I see one yellow mound erupt
in fans and stars and arms
of a monster who yells "trick or treat."

Somewhere they swaddle my newborn son
in gauze and plaster, try to straighten
the bones that bent inside my womb.

It's almost dark when they bring him to me,
the plaster still warm.
The casts turn cold as I hold him
against my stone breast

while children clatter on cobblestones,
circling General Stuart
in their dimestore disguises.

II. In the Nursery

Locked into knotted bone
by a flawed code
you were born
like the black child
with evil connotations.

Like the snake
whose beauty can't compensate:
he will never play it straight.

Nothing straight about you.
Under the baby skin
you're gnarled as a sinister tree.
You'll walk if at all
with the awkward crab.

You share words that describe
with the crooked man,
the twisted mind,
the warped, the wicked.

Oh who can ever straighten you out?

A cramped fist to God for crippled things,
for all things clotted and kinked.

I look at you
and my own dark knots can't be undone.

III. A Birthday

Legs braced in metal,
a pillowcase ghost,
you kick the new ball
fall laughing
into the pile of maple leaves.

Your brown eyes shine
with points of light
like the jack-o'-lanterns
we just lit.

Your sister pulls you up,
your brother ties helium balloons
to your useless wrists.

For one frozen moment I'm certain
you'll rise and float away.

Let go, let go
you have to say
before I even know
I have pinned your golden head
to my heart.

Safeway

This world is category. Raw meat
In slick clear film does not insinuate
Its bloody flesh into meringue-topped sweet
Potato pie. Dark beer and milk don't mate
In this geometry. The Safeway's grid
Defines my need: aisle B the bread, white wine
On C, detergent stacked to pyramid.
The orange and onion never cross their line.
So how come this crippled child bisects my path?
Careens his wheelchair, jerks his body. Why
Does he cock his heavy head at me and laugh
With such strange glee? I can't meet his eye.
I came to this sane place to be alone,
To choose my food, to buy it, to go home.

Stillness Like This

It's stillness that gets you,
not a dingy Greyhound leaving at dawn,
grinding to somewhere strange.
But sit very still in a familiar diner,
expect no one.
Such times you'll feel like a building.

Even leaving you was motion—
your car, then
three airports, two planes, a taxi.
The pilot pointed out Manhattan, Ellis Island.
When we passengers leaned together to look,
the plane tipped to the left. And flying
low over Maryland it cast a shadow
sharp as a sparrow hawk cruising the cornfield.

But what gets you is stillness like this,
lying awake before birds sing to light.
No one is breathing in this house except me.
Out at the curb my car is parked in stone.

Waiting for You

Tiger, when I was fleet
and could leap and sprint
a hundred miles an hour
you never lifted your lazy eyes
or your shaggy head above the grasses.

Now my haunch leaks drops of blood
on the blades you'll move through.

My pores taint the air
to lead you my lame way.

I know
before you do
that I am trapped in your stalking.

Your eyes will bead
on the clues of my wound.
Your nostrils will tighten around my smell.
You will rise and stripe
the yellow grass.

Tiger, you'll move with the stride of a tyrant.
Slowly, toward a sure thing.

Seasons

Sunburned, you cast across the surf
off Hatteras, reeling in the blues.
Your deft flicks—I wanted to kiss
the tendons in your wrist.

At night we fried the fish in butter.
Your body was so beautiful, so hot
and briny to my tongue.

By dove season the sun still burned
in the stubbled fields.
We unpacked the pouch of your sweaty vest,
sat on stools ripping handfuls of feathers
from the warm birds. Our kitchen thickened
with gray down that rose like smoke
around us.

When it was cold enough for geese
you couldn't go. You pressed my palm
against your chest and cried. It's barbed,
you said, this hook in here.
The surgeon's word was *riddled.*

The cedar leans from its tricky stand.
I've pricked my finger stringing berries,
rub my eyes against my wrist.
Tommy struggles with the tangled lights—
goddamn, he says in the voice that wants
to be yours.
Hush, I warn. But I know you
don't hear from upstairs.

You're moving slowly through snow
over Roanoke Ridge

holding the shotgun
before you with both hands.
The berry-fat grouse drums once from the hemlock.
You raise your gun, his wings lift for flight.

Volcanic

Like night coming on the wrong way
the cinder cloud from Mount St. Helens
crosses the continent from west to east.

Earth turns backward and today, here
in Virginia, it seems earlier
than anywhere else in the country.

At noon the lake reflects our fishing poles.
The sunstruck dragonflies couple and hum.
When you say we're getting younger every minute
your eyes are as clear as this air.

Even so, Montana is dark.
Twilight is coming to Kansas,
shadow to the Appalachians.
Before long I'll look at your bare shoulders
and see the fine ash there.
And my hand on the gunnel gloved in dust.

UFO Off the Coast of Maine

You jump up, try to pull me away.
It's frightening, something I've never seen,
can't fit with any name.

Is it something coming to get us?

But what if that sourceless beam of light
aimed straight at the rock we sit on is
something coming
to take us right now, together, out of this world?

This has been a day that burst into our tent
from the Atlantic, the sun splintering mica
off of the rocks, out of the grayest wave.

Morning of woodsmoke, then our gradually warming
skin. We unlayered ourselves to July—
sweaters, then flannels, then everything
except our hands on each other.

In the last violet light we layered ourselves
again, sat in the grass drinking cold beer.
When the stars came out
we walked down here to sit on this flat rock.

I'm old enough to guess how many days like this are left.

As this unearthly light moves closer
I'd just as soon stay still.
Come here. Come sit back down beside me.

Island Life

Between two birches on a hill
I hang out the clothes and pretend
I'm a sailor's wife.

Because as I wrestle
the wet double sheets to the line
they remind me of sails

and when the frayed rope dips
with the weight of the sheets
I can see the boats in Casco Bay.

The big ship rounding Headlight
Point returns, I know,
from Nova Scotia.

I fork the pillowcase corners
with the knobbed wooden prongs
that came with the house

and pretend that you're a sailor.
That's why you packed this morning,
banged the door and rowed for Portland.

Now you could be at the pier with your duffle,
stuffed with the gear your woman
cleaned and folded.

You could be waiting to board the *Scotia Prince*.
You could be looking across to our island,
watching the sails of your laundry catch the wind.

Fall Jazz

Wynton Marsalis' trumpet called down the walls
at the concert, and I'm driving home with a sound
in my head like another country's siren. Stopped
at the tollgate I toss in my quarter and wait
for the flimsy barrier to shudder and lift.

Vapor-lit lanes of the Downtown Expressway double
at the bright row of tollbooths, then narrow
to thread the underpass, emerge alongside the wall
of the Spring Street Prison, where the lights
in an acre of windows have been put out for the night.

Marsalis' horn in the coliseum could have swept
the city like the beam of a truck-mounted searchlight
and found the cell of the man who stared down
at his enormous hands when I rose and said
We find the defendant guilty, Your Honor.

Guilty of attempting to break out of Spring Street
with a weapon he fashioned from pieces of sink
he'd wrenched from the concrete wall with his hands.
By tonight he'd be back on his bunk and aware
of the passage of traffic on the Downtown Expressway.

And the intermittent wail of a trumpet's sweep.
He cups one curved hand over a fist in front
of his lips and blows on his thumb,
fingering the stops of air. He's alone,
I know, because that's what we sentenced him to.

At home, I let myself in through the kitchen,
click on the floodlight and lean toward the window
over my sink. Out there the crickets insist
like jazz. The last chrysanthemums stand hack
by the fence, violet at the edge of the light.

Caravati's Junkyard

Dried sinks and hot
iceboxes squat on
the chickweed.
Fireless mantels
gape from a shed.

Doors without houses
lean still and stiff
on Caravati's fence.
Doors without handles
unhinged in the sun
peel to their
useful wood.

Beyond stacks of
banisters, past
piles of wrought
iron railings,
in an empty
ragweed lot,
one door stands up

closing on Caravati's
Junkyard, opening
on goldenrod,
hinging on air.

All My Friends' Pets Are Growing Old

All my friends' pets are growing old.
Mike's clawless, scabby cat can't roam outside
for fear the bluejays she once mocked will strike
and peck her sores. So Mike picks up the turds
from his prize rugs with only mild disgust
and smiles at Tiger sleeping in a shaft of sun.
Barbara said at lunch the other day she's lugging
her black Lab (with help to push him up
into the car) weekly to the vet's for shots
and every Tuesday he plays dead at two o'clock.
I thought how much I'd hate a week with such a time
tied to it. I didn't like her dog when
he was frisky. I did like Millie's Corgi
who looked old when he was new, but I hate
the way she talks now of his cancer
as if he were a relative or friend.
Bob and Connie Kincaid are the worst
with their menagerie—a house that reeks of cat
piss, two huge wheezing dogs—one with heart-
worm—a hamster worn to lumpenness from running round
in circles, a toothless rabbit, Aphrodite,
they coax to suck a bottle. And talk,
that's all they do is talk of all the trouble
they go to, so smug the way they're trying to
suggest they'd do the same for anyone. And the part
I really cannot bear, they trick me
into talking about Whitlock Street, where
we couples stood around somebody's small backyard,
grilling sirloins, sipping beer, a nudge or hug
to go with watching Millie's puppy waddle
grass-high toward the plump legs of our diapered babies.

Beyond Recognition

A lesion that destroys this area of the cerebral cortex impairs
the ability to identify a person by facial features.
   —*Scientific American*

And though there is no sudden face
in the doorway that makes you rush
to touch its familiar cheek,
neither is there the face
that causes you to cringe
or triggers the wish to smash it.

The leering face in the kitchen window
you couldn't erase from dreams
since you were eight,
the face you never could unmask
yet live with on a vow,
the wrinkled woman in your mirror,

all are innocent of history
as this problem child who comes to visit.

You ask me every time
in that same expectant voice

Now who are you?

January Flies

Such moist warmth, such insistent
rhythm must have spawned them—
the furnace basso harrumphing off, on, off,
on against these zero nights, the laundry's
hot wet water, hot dry air, cycle on cycle,
steam fuzzing up the walls like lush mold—
a fly could hardly resist being born.

When I opened the basement door I gasped
and slammed it on a scene from a disaster flick:
a swarm of fat black flies bobbing up the stairway
toward my face.

Since then I'm bent on annihilation,
gassings through the cracked door. For three
who made it through I raised a window,
watched them drone to a freedom
where the garbage is frozen. I found one
floating, glistening black in my son's milk.

Tonight there's one more left. The fittest,
I suppose, has made it up another flight, survives
in my bedroom. This fly is delirious.
With death, I don't know, with the perfume
in my room? With some sense the time's all wrong?

It flings its fizzing blood against the windowpane
and I come at it with a rolled magazine, inflamed
out of proportion, vertiginous as a January fly.

Luncheon of the Boating Party

Long before he had to strap the brushes
to his wrists, Renoir had stolen time.
He'd learned a way to preserve afternoons,
glint sun on crystal by laying on pure white,
distill white wine with dabs of ocher.
And a thick black line can set an awning flapping.

It's true that falling sun lights crystal.
Under Catherine's awning in Indian summer
the rose hips glow against the low brick wall.
I preserve them, she says, reaching behind her
languidly to pick one. Paul's bare forearm rests
on the tablecloth. My fingers uncurl
from the stem of the wineglass and spread
until my little finger touches the fine hair
on his wrist. A crumpled napkin lies between
the empty emerald bottle and the amber one.

Renoir posed his brawny friends in sleeveless shirts,
used blue to bulge the muscles in their upper arms.
For him the girl he loved held still
until the sun was right, on her rounded cheek,
on Brett's straw hat, on the folds of white linen.

William knuckles the ears of his arching cat, tells
one last summer story. Our laughter's as low
as the rumbling purr, as the breeze fluttering
the scalloped awning. Paul is watching Catherine
crush the rose hip. William's smiling drowsily at me.

And yet, at forty-one, Renoir disdained this painting
and all his other art. "I have forgotten,"
he wrote to Brett, "how either to paint or to draw,"

and in 1882 he left for Rome to study the frescoes
of Raphael. Critics today prefer his late work,
its more formal concerns, its rich paint. In the last
paintings the human body becomes almost abstract.

THE GOVERNOR OF DESIRE

Ungovernable

Trying to counter it
is pitiful as sandbags—
filling the burlap in heavy rain,
lugging the wet bags to the edges,
shoving them up.
It makes you sigh it's so useless,
so heavy, so difficult to shore
the meager barricade against this mystery.

Here it comes, gathered from the snow fields,
the high and hidden springs, the long rains.
Here it is, ungovernable,
overwhelming the reasoned dams,
those useless lumps.

And of course we knew it all along, that lantern-
lit night, our wet work in the dark . . .

It's going to be the talk for years
along the river towns
and if we get out of this alive
the day will come
we'll shake our heads and smile,
our lips shaping the word *survived*
like a kiss.

Do You or I or Anyone Know

What is this way of gods: how they go?
Down, down below the ground, into the world
our old stories try to show
where life is detained for winter, or forever,
down a god will go
before you know it. Or up, ascension,
into emblazoned clouds, into spun dust.

Our arts, those scraps of history's yardage,
report vanishings
though no one actually sees which way gods go.

No, what the woman sees is almost the same
in all the stories: a handful of feathers,
a dust of gold, a tree trunk or stone rolled
back from the only way out. The strange baby
she will never explain.

Laws of Nature

The moment hangs now,
Snapped at the stem
Not by her, not by him.
They claim by weight it left the bough.

It stops in air until they meet
This Friday, then will fall
Into their hands, their mouths; all
Our laws, they'll sigh, are round and sweet.

Do You Remember Where You Were?

"I Wanna Hold Your Hand" smacked a slap
of off-accustomed beat at Three Chopt Road
and Grove. Like Hopkins' wrung-wrought half
beats butting into iambic business, Beatles
stuck it to my radio and my stop-lit ear
drummed oh and no and o and kay. And oh now
it's so old, so memory lane . . .

On Three Chopt Road I knew like news
of assassination this music shoot was a shake-
down crashcourse. Skulls would crack,
this decade'd be no easylistening, this assault
a worldall one. Even beats got bullets then,
blasts from barricades who knows where now,
blood all over everybody's car, *ka-pow, ka-pow, pow.*

Mother's Side

Red hair, red hair, and that pale skin
that cannot bear six minutes in the sun—
what have I to do with those green eyes,
whiskey-dazed, dream-dimmed, and oh,
the O's initiating names
of the potato poor in America?
What's my connection to Celtic song,
priests of unreason, the scream of wrath
from another room, sensual laughter
somewhere outside in the long night?

I with my big Belgian nose, my hair,
my eyes as dark as the fathers
always gaining or losing ground around them
(Bruges, Ardennes, all of Georgia), always
thinking.

I am tall, I am darkhaired, I take apart myth.
But there are nights beyond reason in August
after even *my* skin has burned, turned red,
when over the hum of the window fan
I hear the owl and the desperate whistle
of his rabbit, the hot breath of cicadas.
I drink long to cool down, to explain away
the other sound burning outside in the dark.

Puritans

More weight!
Giles Corey ordered.
The Puritans heaved another gray stone
slab upon his chest—
yet could not press confession.
Before he died, he said again
More weight.

So far from Salem
these brown mountains loom,
her Puritan jury.
Above the sliced-out pass to Aspen
the sodden clouds bear down.
Boulders are moving in
on the narrowing highway.
Their closed car squeezes the air to stones.

Her chest rises to each breath
as she dreams of the face of the stranger,
feels again his strange weight.

A Summer Lover's Book

I lean my face onto the words he wrote,
smelling ink and pine and sun on skin,
then crack the new book's spine to lay if flat
and now I'm on the tree-loft floor

where planks of pine across the forked mimosa
smell like paper, fresh cream vellum,
open, sunwarmed books. The fretty leaves
play up and down the page with light,
shifting fringe of shadow on the words.

"She's up in the mimosa tree," they'd say
those summer days my bones grew long.
"Her nose is always buried in some book."
"Never does a lick," they'd say,
"lazy as they come."

But lazy didn't matter then
as long as I could read and leave Atlanta,
uncurling like a newborn from the cramp
of time and space I was a child in,
the embarrassment of hours inside the house.

Limbs I lay on, subtle motion of the boughs,
urged the friction I could find in print.
With a puff of pink mimosa I could tickle
my warm skin and if the book were new I'd bend
my face into the pungence of its ink

then raise my head and slowly let the focus
come, let the words begin to work in me,
confusing as I always have the source of poetry:
places words have taken me, places where I've been;
touching a real cheekbone, reading in trees.

What Is the Most Elvis Ever Weighed?

I guess I could say the answer begins
the day in our storeroom I took shotgun shells
from their cardboard box and fingered the rough
red paper and round brassy bottoms, rolled
their dual weights in the palm of my hand, then
stood them side by side in the medicine cabinet
of the basement bathroom—that was the heaviest
medicine I could imagine.
Did I know how to crack and load and fire? No.
Did I mean it? I don't know. Did the King
mean to weigh two hundred and sixty?
That's the answer to the quiz on my car radio.

Backstage at the Fox he was so thin
and young he knew no need or need to hide
from sex-sent sixteen-year-old girls.
He welcomed us unguarded then and Carly
Anne sat on his lap. He laughed
and let his slender fingers dimple her bare arms,
while my hand moved to touch the curve of his guitar
that glittered on the chair beside me.
He opened a Co-cola with his keyring
and offered it around. *I sure am happy,* he said once,
pronouncing *I* the way we did, almost like *awe.*
What's next! said Carly Anne, who planned ahead.
Oh, I don't know, said Elvis. *Let's go see y'all's folks.*
And so we did, his eyes and ours darkwide and shining,
ready to watch the weighty world come on.

Heart's Core

It's a difficult nut to crack.

Like splitting the atom,
once done, men and
women in starched coats step back,
afraid of what they'd craved:

>   box of unbelievables
>   blows its lid—
>   energies spew, spiral,
>   boil into every corner—
>   the yeasty porridge crowds the house.

Prodigal fission! Too much!
Too dangerous to concentrate,
to take deliberate aim
at the heart of a human target.

We settle for charged air
over oceans, fallout
on empty atolls—

>   exploding only
>   the golden fish,
>   blasting unseen fragile valves.

The Uninvestigated Stanza

Phrase coined by Helen Vendler in *New York Review of Books*

In Italy stanza means rooms.
But she speaks of poetry, demanding the nerve
it takes a poet to look into the words,
to check and check again the apartments of the poem.

Listen: if it takes a tumbler pressed against the wall,
listen like a gossip or a spy.
Or with your ear where the plumbing meets the floor,
listen for cries. For
if the poem fails to investigate
the rooms next door, the story below,
the scream that sounds like a trapped animal
will become a trapped animal.

A cat, say, and not a child.

The smack of thin bones in a small head
against ceramic tile
will diminish to a cringe
in a corner of the stanza
written off
with words

like, "heard a door slam in the distance . . ."

And if a poem can baffle
the sounds in its building,
something hard can prod into tenderness
while a pillow presses off
the cries
and we can turn up the volume, practice surprise
to greet the investigator knocking now
loud, and louder, at our door.

Sounds that Have Gone from Our Lives

Listen! You can hear it now—the acoustic
lawn mower from my neighbor's yard:

it sounds like *churr* only as long as she pushes,
mostly short jabs around her trees.

The sound's almost as soft as a carpetsweeper,
bicycle tires in the driveway, the eggbeater

doing its three hundred turns in the batter
in a big yellow pottery bowl, then the clinks

of the hand-washed dishes, the snap of sheets
and drying shirts flapping in the wind,

the firewood mounting slowly to the rasp
and re-rasp of the handheld saw.

Women pumping silent Singer treadles,
women fanning cardboard scenes of Jesus,

quietly sewed the seams and cooled the church.
Once things went without us they got loud

and covered over snores and slaps and prayers,
cries of pain and quiet sobbing on the stairs.

The Place You Left

I'm leaning again in my doorway
here in the sun that is merely the place
where the sun used to be.

The silence is surfaced by usual noise—
woodpecker in Ollie's pasture,
the Norfolk & Southern's morning clatter.

The emptiness is spotted with objects
you will remember: dome of blue sky,
fat bees, pink rock holding open the door.

There are still some things to touch—
a sculpted egg, thistle pods, my cheek
against my fingertips.

Instead of dog, walnut, lemon,
there's more lilac now.
But even that sweetness is just a place
where lilac used to be.

Branches

Somewhere in here it's there, in a tributary
of circuitry, among the jungled arbors,
the ramifications of the heart—
it's the forked road up the mountain
it's the dirt road to the left
and then
way back in the pale light of April
against dark and leafless hardwood branches
the dogwood flashes white
shines briefly like your eyes
on me when I looked up the night
of the lightning
my darkened room
the doorway open to the light show
clicking and branching its quick veins
into the silhouettes of limbs
of trees attracting lightning
to the ground until one cracked
and fell for you to saw its branch
into a seat that swings now
back and forth
from this bough in my mind
somewhere in here among the jungled arbors
decked with your imagery like intricate mosses
and myriad gifts of bower birds.

What Turns the Wheel of Fortune

A thousand people come out of their cottages
to watch the governor pass,
to sigh at his charmed life, his lovely children,
their yellow curls, their blue velvet jackets.

The golden spokes of his carriage wheels
spin so easily they seem to stay still.
And yet he is passing, passing them by
to the music of trumpets and drums.

He's gone, and one woman goes in to her child
who can't breathe through the clotted phlegm
that came from nowhere. Men go back
to the fields to bend again over fruit
their strawboned children never see.
And the woman standing by the linden
will be hanged next week for whispering.

When the day comes the governor hears
something slip underneath—rumors of war,
of outlawed origins, of errors made in love
he thought he'd paid for—
when he hears a little screech and feels
a forward jerk of the wheel he stands on,

he shouldn't look to Heaven or to Fate
or necessarily take on all the blame.
A thousand people in their cottages working
with the basest metals we've been given—
envy, bitterness, a misunderstanding of wheels—
have welded the lever to start things rolling.

Czechoslovakia, 1989

There was something so lovely about the way
she ducked her head, light brown bangs touching
her eyelashes. When she walked across
the room, we could see she was almost a woman,
her breasts now points under thin jersey,
her hips as narrow as a boy's but beginning to move
like a woman's. She wore a tennis player's skirt
that flipped against her long pale thighs.

Boys and girls, we loved her voice. Shy
as a child, she stood beside the ragtag band
and sang the songs that she and I had written.
Her low notes rose from somewhere lonely
we hadn't known to name. I think now
she turned our words to yearning to be owned.

For soon the boys began their circling in
the parking lot, lowering like stags, clashing
in muffled thuds that underscored the music.
One night I watched the feisty one come in,
stride to the bandstand and circle her wrist
with his fingers. I saw them leave together
before her song was over.

There was another after him, but time
(I heard three years) between them when she sang
for pleasure in little clubs in Prague.
Then I saw her picture in the paper with a man—
this time one hand was on her neck, his other
on her arm. They seemed to smile,
but I had learned by then to read the meaning
of shadowed dents on fingered skin.

And since those shadows, all these sunless years.
We're not young now, no. A joke we would have

giggled over in the park, aging ladies acting young.
I hear she's thrown him out and sings as if
she knows what she will do. I'm going to see.

What if she's forgotten, or what if we
have learned a thin-lipped laugh?
Will she remember summer nights the boys
locked horns in parking lots? Will she remember
how she sang the come-and-get-me songs
we didn't know we'd written?

Sunset on Eastern Beaches

In Tuscany we sat for seven evenings
facing west, as the biggest sun we'd ever seen
suffused the sky in hues we hadn't dreamed of
and the fired horizon hushed us into silence.

On a Key West pier we watched the sun go down
as a black man beat a steel drum slowly.
Awed by ritual, we joined in the applause
as the sun's red rim was sucked into the Gulf.

But the last light on eastern beaches
does not command response. Here on Nag's Head
the air is washed. The sand turns gold.
The whitecaps flap like sunbleached flags
and clean cottons we wear down now
from the cottages after our showers.

Calling to one another, carrying babies
and sandals and iced lime drinks, we go down
to the edge of water. Our faces glow with sun
we cannot see. Our children splash in tidal pools,
their sandy bodies shining.

Matthew in Uniform

Nights in the late sixties
after the 6:30 news of the war,
I put Matt to bed propped
against pillows
so he could breathe.

He'd sink into his baby chins,
smile at me and fall asleep.
He hardly ever cried.

But he made a noise
in the middle of most nights
that was a mix of gasp and mucus.

I'd bring him to the rocking chair,
his feet kneading my stomach, his chin
bearing on my collarbone.

His breathing would slow
to the rocker's rhythm, my throaty songs—
Baez, Dylan, Saigon Bride,
Where have all the soldiers gone?

And one song of my own that went
*I'd hide Matt in the basement, I'd hide
Matt in the attic, I'd put Matt back
inside me if he had to go to war.*

Now here is Matthew. As Homer sang,
my tall son is standing in the door.
Matthew in uniform, chest full of breath.
His chin juts above the stiff collar.

I wish I could hold him, hide him.
I wish I could hide him from the gleam
of the sun on trumpets, the spangled banners,
the shine of a mother's mongering pride.

Define Space

Space in the brain
between axon and dendrite
is open to possibility
as Michelangelo left the famous space
between Adam's fingertip and God's.

The same as the empty box
a day makes on a calendar,
the wedge of shadow on the sundial's circle
seems only lack of light, but tells
us what we need to know of time.

Space is not what is not,
nor the object of rockets;
it's the way they get where they're going.
It's the cold blue absence of you
that bristles me into the future.

Space is the lively medium—
that made-up lady we have trouble believing,
who goes into a trance of not-being,
rolls her eyes toward the place
where you could have gone
and asks us all here to hold hands.

Define Time

The cool blues trumpet sweet
and sad, gray and grainy
photographs of a fifties' trip,
the Rainbow Room in one turn of a boy's arms
spins above a billion nightlights,
a princess child whirls into the real dream,
the most magic I'd ever conjured: a woman.
Saxophone smoke in the Village and then
so young, so merry, we ride to an island
and lean on the railing amazed at ourselves.
Senses invade the caves of my brain, now
I smell the garbage and orange juice, see
crescents of soot under my nails, steam
of first coffee city dawn, November '56.
We stay awake for days and nights and kiss
in the corridors and courts of the Plaza,
embrace in our camel's-hair coats
on the platform of Grand Central Station.
I was seventeen, I am seventeen, there is
no such time called seventeen,
there is no such thing as time.

Loss Without Ceremony

That hunger in the gut no one cooks for,
comes by to sign for, to cry for, no one comes
to sit up all night on the sofa saying *yes*
yes I remember so well, here, you ought to eat—

this is the most jagged grief,
emptiness unmourned by any rite.

Not the crowded kitchen
where we sat at her mother's wood table
after the service
with her aunt and Tom and her wordless son.
We were, of all things, peeling potatoes
and chopping onions. *A ridiculous recipe*
we sniffled over our knives,
slicing into the sheer layers.

Later the dishes, the running
water, scraping, steam,
the clink and clank and churn,
the balletic action of passing
from one to the other. I bumped
into her son, who smiled. I touched
her husband's wrist. Over his dark
blue suit, he had on a crazy apron.

Mary Anne can't find a vase
for the lilacs. Can Alec go for ice?
Did somebody bring some bourbon?
I'll go next door to Lola's.

It isn't any consolation, said someone young
who hadn't lived through loss without a ceremony.
Who hadn't been a man who lost a man he loved in secret.
Or one who from the window watched a moving van back out.
Or one who loves a child whose eyes have turned to walls.

All you can do is walk slowly through a stubbled field,
pick some Queen Anne's lace,
listen to the crickets.
And wish you were in a kitchen
polishing silver, washing dishes,
making something with your friends.

ON LONG MOUNTAIN

Perseid Night

The storm of stars predicted
can't break this clouded sky, so in my
pulled-up chair on Long Mountain
I give up the sight—and begin to hear
the storm of sounds that pelt the air:
chirp and drill and drum and vibrato,
rhythmic rasp and blue-note howl.
Meteors of messages
trace quick arcs across me.
Now and then a barking dog
from down at Bluford's. And I understand
the crickets, a cow's low call, mosquito whine.
But it's so dark to a city girl
sitting out here to see stars—
What makes a shriek? a chuff? a tinny cry?
Who is signaling, what is signed?
Are any getting answers beneath this no-show heaven?

Unarmed

Get a gun was what was offered
as advice
by all but the closest friend
who said
You'd shoot yourself. Out of stupidity.
Or sadness.

In the Blue Ridge Mountain cabin loft
lying awake alone
I stare at the timbered ceiling
—and because I believed her—
fight fear unarmed.

For a long time the bear
scratched her nails on the windowpane,
muffled her thumps at the door,
shifted her shape under barnlight.

So too the hiker crazed for the food
of my flesh, swings my rust-hinged gate,
scrapes his knife against the tin roof,
strangles soft things into tiny shrieks.

While the snake, the copperhead,
slides along the rafter,
dangles over my head in my fitful sleep,
eases back into shadow when I jerk awake and reach

for the gun
that I never got, so much more afraid
of stupidity, of sadness.

Gnat Facts on NPR

Now I know for sure
every living thing springs
for sex. Gnats
swarming in your face,
snuffing up your nose
guttering in the liquid of your eye—
they're doing a fucking *dance!*
Their aerial male fandango's as hot
as Watusi writhing in fireheat,
as white boys oiling their torsos
to volley a ball at Fort Lauderdale.
"They orient themselves to a tall pole,"
says here—which is you, in June,
gnat-exasperated, batting hot air—
"and if that pole moves—they go with it."
Down the graveled walk by the black walnut
where you wanted to talk, to maybe touch,
but you're fanning your sweaty face,
your lips are sealed.
It's all for the females,
says the expert, that "hang back on the sidelines
until the frenetic cloud of their kind
is too much to resist." Then they jump in—
mate right there in your shut-down face.

It's the radio's word *sidelines*
switches the picture to cold Friday nights,
the sidelines swaying to rhythmic cheers,
the scrimmagers wild in a flurry of motion's
sounds: tackle and crack and knocked-out wind.
Then something signals us girls. A buzzer, a gun,
and it's time to run
onto the field, into the thick, grab the boys tight
around stiff plastic pads, thin padded hips,
knowing their swarming is all about *us,*
loving the sweat they drip.

Blues in the Blue Ridge

On the year's hottest day
Wynton Marsalis trumpets a dirge
over the burial beat
of a New Orleans drum.

Under the clicking ceiling fan
I'm reading Euripides,
sweating in my white nightgown,
the thinnest cotton I brought up here
to pass this time alone.
The fan sends its heated breeze
to my wicker chair.

It's afternoon in August; in Argos
Electra is mourning her father,
keening her dark lamentation,
her rhythmical, murderous song.

This bleaching sun in Virginia
bears down on the mountainside,
the grass is as dry and as dun as Mycenae's.
Goldfinches fight over thistle. Sunflowers glare.
In this thick air my thin batiste gown
sticks to the sides of my breasts.
I can barely move
in the heat and light of grief
as mourners in New Orleans wail
in hot black suits and blues.

Sensing Winter

Four narcissus blooms, browning
paper-whites forced for Christmas,
assert their scents like skunks
on the cold night parkway.
In a small apartment there's no doubt
what wins among the senses.
The silent telephone smells
like plastic when the handle of a pan
melts over the burner turned to high.
The woman stretches out of her sweater,
unbuttons her wool skirt that falls
around her feet. She hooks her thumbs
into her pantyhose, watches her body
becoming naked in the mirror
propped against a wall. She shivers in
the forced-air heat and for a second
she can smell her skin, its sweetness.
But her own odor won't linger here,
faint as the tentative fingertip
she touches to her self.

Can't You Hear Me Singing, Alfred Prufrock?

I watched you today in my mind's eye—
walk down the stairs,
your rumpled pants rolled at the ankle
your bald spot round as a target.
You were going. And what's more,
dying. Or going
to die. *Wait!* I yelled,
I'm going too!
You stopped, popeyed as a lobster:
Do I understand just what you mean?
Of course, I said, and in an instant
we were sitting
in an orchard on Long Mountain
laughing, dying
laughing and eating
peaches, touching each
other with warm sticky fingers.

Willem de Kooning Declared Incompetent

news item, August, 1989

Experts sent to inspect him assert
he can't tell the difference between one and a million.
But "de Kooning continues to paint every day."

In conversation he roamed from the subject
of money. It's all potatoes
Willem de Kooning declared, incompetent.

He looks out at the level potato field,
at the straight line it makes with the Long Island sky
and the line that it doesn't make with the sky—
the line of his mind that he makes as de Kooning
continues to paint
every day.

Ways to Go

> Let us go then you and I . . .
>   —T. S. Eliot

> There's a hell of a good universe next door;
>   Let's go!
>   —e.e. cummings

> Let's go to Gubbio tonight.
>   —William Matthews

How casually poets and people use
"Let's go"—as if it were a given
that someone else will want to.

On the drive to Gubbio, she'll sigh
at that sunset behind the ancient towers
and hills of Tuscany. He'll feel, with her hand on
his thigh, it's okay to think about religion
and her breasts rounded above the peasant blouse.

Not that "Let's go" is always a poet's dream.
The pasta could be at Joe's on Route 1,
or the words sighed by two
who're bored with Chesterfield County.
They may even be bored with each other
as they open the doors to their car.

But the singular construction cannot invite
a soul to come along.
Its whole tone is joyless,
breaking someone's hold, insisting
on leaving for Italy alone.

Her words still ring in the roadway:
"Let me go, let me go."

Like Young Men

It's hard not to love
the way they stand, easy and affirmed
like young men alone together
not knowing they're watched.

A sweetness in their power, a hesitancy.
One stag lowers his head to my garden.
The other, calmly alert, looks to this cabin.

They take turns protecting each other
in a beautiful simplicity of eating and guarding.
Their clay-colored bodies are a massive surprise
after the delicate doe I've chased from here.

Their racks are young, but sharpening. It's hard
not to stare, not to freeze. The guardian
arouses the other to a scent of harm
that could be me—

his antlers toss and almost instantly
both deer bound up the hill,
take my fence with ease,
lithe and cocky as teenagers, armed.

Painting the Blue Ridge Red

Art class assignment: use opposite hues.
So undulant mountains,
blued by the haze their humid greens give off,
are red as ocean rollers in a sunrise.
Look at my bluebird almost orange
and that ripening corn—a mustard field.
I'll make the lilac brown and tinge
the cows with pink. The chinking
of the cabin I'll turn purple.
But wait awhile, Long Mountain paints
this exercise itself: cadmium trees,
alizarin ridges. Lilac dries to burnt sienna,
the greens of summer go to ochre.
The Goldfinch molts to gray.
In winter light, the cabin
casts its violet shadow. Here
no color can surprise a canvas
except crow's constancy.

Leaving the Butterfly Bush

You have to have seen one to know at first
the eight-foot bush isn't full of windwaved flames
or shards of thin stained glass
firing the sunlight to orange and gold.

The monarchs are migrating,
gathering in the Blue Ridge to feast and fill
on aster and goldenrod and especially buddleia,
the fragrant violet butterfly bush.
They'll fatten in late summer sun, then fly
three thousand miles to Mexico.

Now among the heavy August greens,
this hillside's dotted with their fluttering
and here and there an early dying leaf,
a thin yellow walnut leaf,
briefly becomes a butterfly.

I want to take a picture of my lively buddleia
for I must go down the mountain now
and when I return the monarchs will have flown,
the purple spikes sucked dry and browned.

But I have no camera—and what if I did?—
it is the movement that amazes.
And no video could do it, missing the scent,
the silence, the feel of the Long Mountain air
on my skin—as if I'm being softly fanned
by a thousand pairs of wings without a sound.

I can't preserve this moment
any more than Moses could—
just watch a bush ignited,
and try to write it down.

Enthusiasm

Possessed by a god
says the word:
god is in.

Sure as a stroke
something spins in the brain,
fluttering the airy layers, taking over,
wreaking redness, wildness,
havoc in the actions.

Someone once made me ashamed of such mania.
It was after I'd had a baby.
Calm down, he said.

Rosy in the possible, I wonder
how the milkwhite understand anything.
They feint, they fend, they
palely duck the blow.

I was beside myself
Euripides wrote
through the voice
of the woman god-possessed.

She's not herself
is what I heard around here.
God—devoutly I wish now
to be pushed aside.

Come on, come in,
knock me out.

Unbalanced

Winter, 1995

Accurate languages
fragged into that side and this
atomized over the damaged maps

this little globe grows
more and more our home
until Chechnya and Zagreb
shadow the optimistic grass
of Gettysburg

and here
unheard of murders
become what one could do

until one night walking
on the swinging bridge thinner than feet
your outstretched upturned palms
depending
as always on even rain
you're surprised by one hand dry.

You would plunge but for poetry
or whatever the better word
for when language composes
the drifting chips of the world's
composure, fills the empty
outstretched hand with flakes
that counterweigh the one with rain.

"Now Words Are Surrounded by Spaces"

—elementary Classical Greek textbook

To me it hadn't occurred
that words were
surrounded by spaces

that once
ancient Greek ran words like pearls
able to touch each other's curves
across the knotted string
each one gleaming
like strung round worlds
by Vermeer

that somewhere
along the line
someone
split words in two like the axed dash
of Emily Dickinson

and now the space that surrounds
a word
can hold it like a star
in darkness
the space between words
can gape and take
my stepping foot to a place
I hadn't planned.

Was it safer when nouns
held on tight
to what moved them through space:
backward or forth
to what lands or latches or catches
or is
an object?

Oh words how unhooked you've become after Greek!
Look at you standing there
side by side
straining so hard to make meaning,
pretending you've never touched.

Nameless

Most all of us came this way.
Muscled through the no-name,
our big heads stretched the holding tight
that still presses our bodies in dreams.

Even the gentle lover finds no object
for his verb to whisper as he enters
the holding tight that presses like his dreams.
The route of his birth and his fathering
is not sealed at the end of his penis,
is neither sheath nor scabbard.

And some who died to tell about it speak
in similes: of darkness like a corridor,
like a tunnel, like a narrow passageway
to brilliance.

They can't compare their going out
with the birth they don't remember,
and even if near death they could,
the route has no true name.

Momentary Travels

I had thought these moments were yours,
these moments when I've left this life
for that other one, I thought you were there too.

That everybody was there. That this
was where you all went
when I couldn't find you.

But I just now suspected you might be
at your own places—not this one
Thelonious Monk drifted me into

before sleep where I'm around midnight,
young and sultry at a corner table
in a dark and smoky jazz club.

In of course New York.
But were you in the Shenandoah Valley
that redbud April afternoon?

There was a trout stream there,
a little stream, but noisy as jazz
in the smoky air of the Blue Ridge.

I've begun to think the sadness
that wells up in me when I return
is that I was never there, myself.

Even in Foxes

Even in foxes
cunning and quickness
curl in on themselves
in the den of that thief, time.

Brain and bones click into pain
in the loose bag dimmed to dun.
Each bristle wilts,
limp as an eyelash.

At the henhouse stupidity clucks
among the young
who misunderstand
the hand that feeds them,

while on the hill the jangling hounds
call out their longing,
sniffing the air, the ground,
confused by the musk of memory.

Poetry Reading

This is my last poem:
pay attention.
I know there were minutes—
whole poems back there—
when I lost you.
I know your mind tried, for a while,
to stay behind your eyes,
but at times, it just had to be excused
as I used to raise my hand and
ask Miss Sanders, *May I?*
And out I'd go, excused
from the overheated room,
the drone of geography, the smell
of bananas in brown paper bags,
and though Tammy tried to come with me
it was always one-at-a-time
just as *your* mind couldn't leave this room
with the mind of that person sitting beside you
(try as you might to invite it along)
but walked down the hall by itself
into that small hotel
where some word I'd spoken
—*hibiscus, vanilla, mahogany, snow*—
reminded you
someone you've missed for a very long time
stands at a window brushing her hair
and hearing you speak her name she turns
her face that has not changed at all
to yours and holds out her arms to encircle your body
which is not there, but here in this room
where you've sat very still and listened
to some if not all of my words
and may or may not have heard
that this is my last poem.

Valdosta

How do I like it here?
I've been young so long, being here
is taking some adjustment. At first
the squared-off lowrise blocks, expected stop-
lights regulating traffic,
the sunlight on brick buildings
looked familiar.
A Hopper afternoon, I thought, or downtown
Valdosta in the fifties.

After a while you get tired of adjusting,
weary so soon on the afternoon errand,
moving with care like one under water, though air
dries your eyes beyond blinking
and the sunlight glares glass into mirrors.

So it's a mystery who's inside cars,
and what's behind storefront windows.
Who is that girl in the tight black shorts
cross-cutting traffic like a lawless god?
The grace of her bare long legs, the freedom
of her unbound breasts! Is she running to that shadow
in the alley? She flings open her arms to something
or somebody there, her reckless hair
glints sun like chrome.

Stopped like everyone else on this street,
I see her quick motion reflect in the glass,
then disappear, and I hate it here, I hate it.

At the End of August

Two cool days turn a few leaves red on one dogwood
and even though every leaf in my yard is green—
maple, azalea, maidenhair fern, ginkgo,
gardenia, pin oak, willow—
these scarlet few are a fingernail
on my shoulderblade.
I turn
to push the duffle into his trunk,
help to hoist the mystery box,
leave all the dollars in my wallet
on the dashboard,
smile red goodbyes
to the packed back, the convivial stickers.
The dust in the driveway drifts toward the trees,
yards full, woods full, all dull green
except that tip of dogwood waving too.

Swing, Boat, Table

What Hanno has made of wood this year:
a swing, a boat, a table.

He doesn't believe he's made art this year;
the swing, the boat, the table

are objects he made to invite those he loves
to sit down.

Not objects people in rooms walk around,
regard in boredom or awe while locked at the knee—

a few vaguely yearning to float to the sea,
break bread with friends, rise through the air—

a few vaguely yearning—and not knowing why—
to sit in a tree.

WITHOUT A PHILOSOPHY

Without a Philosophy

... like a dog between 4 trees ...
—e-mail from a friend

Toward the end of this summer,
this long labyrinth,
I thought of you in a clearing
green and sunlit, bordered by four
tall trees and the dusky spaces
between them where barely
discernible rhododendron
start the process of shadows.

Light moves on your turning
shoulders and on the four tall trees:
the black walnut, the copper beech,
two sycamores peeling to bonewhite
the sun loves most.

It's not only the trees but more
than your fabled dog's choices;
it's those darknesses between
that like me, you are lured to choose.

But you are arrested there—
watching the swallowtails
feed on the aster, then go in
and disappear.

Diagnosis, after Dickinson

Increments of information
Slant upward from the shock
That forms the quadrilateral fact—
Base of solid rock

Increments of information
Slowly pyramid—
We're either learning more each day
Or slantedly misled

Increments of information
Are all that we can bear—
Giving hope of pinnacle
While pointing to the air

Bombing Yugoslavia

Blue Ridge Mountains, April 1999

Goldfinches squabble for the broken peg
perch at the thistle-seed feeder. Blood-
red cardinals fight for territory
in the forsythia hedge—redder than ever
against that gold explosion
waving its tendrils in uncertain sun.
For now the winds are massing clouds,
gray rollers on the ridges to the east.

The groundhog's up and out and down,
undermining everything.
I can push a rock against his hole
but it's hopeless, he'll get around it
like the poison ivy's early shoots
that won't be stopped by any herbicide
I spray, no nipping this one in the bud, its invasion
is accomplished by July.
Meadow grass has sprung above surprises
and you have to walk with care across it now.
Ground bees are up. The snake's awake.
The snake, in fact, I saw today and shuddered;
its head was in the bluebirds' house.
Its long tail dangled out the augured hole.

Out here planting lilies at the border,
I'm struck by blood
along the blue vein of my wrist.
A jagged rock? A barb of buried wire?
It's blood I've come here to forget, fought
the thoughts all day: your open chest in Boston,
the roadsides out of Kosovo.

The Well

They stride in garish clothes—dayglow
orange, purple fleece, tweeds—nothing
matches. Their voices babble and clash
in cacophony nobody hushes.

Most drive their bodies like madmen,
perpetrating purpose, cells
to their ears, striding the streets
straight ahead.

Though there are some who saunter
with no protocol,
with the brainless insouciance
of all the time in the world.

There is no reason
for their delusion, their lack of decorum.
Unfazed by fact, they go about
their suspicious business.

Struck by sun, not one
of the well ever looks up
here to the hospital window,
even shading his eyes with his hand.

Shutters

Through the slanted louvers, light
cracks the shadowed room; October
Sunday afternoon asserts its life.
Slats of brightness on your blanket
insist the sky outside is cold blue.

Your cheeks would redden like leaves
if only you could rise and come outside.
We could breathe bracing, electric air.
We could walk,
walk fast to keep warm
because there's a chill out there in the park
though the grass is still green
and most of the trees here in Louisville
haven't faced the fact of frost. I can't sit still,
leafing *The Times* as you lie there.
Its pages litter the light-barred floor.

But who am I to feel so stuck inside,
for we both know the truth
that when we were young I spent
so many golden Sunday afternoons
in shuttered rooms. Crack a cold beer
and oh how we loved shutting out the sun,
some football game droning
its thudding plays beneath our breathing.

Drawing Lesson: Outline and Edge

> An outline surrounds a form that is no longer there.
>   —Eleanor Rufty

Like this drawing by my mother of my baby hand,
the plump, splayed fingers outlined in waxy crayon.

Or the body on the sidewalk:
here's where it was when it fell.
Flat blue chalk shows he raised his hands.

Where is the form no longer there?
If auras of angels were outlines
who knows where the angel flew?
Or the victim, bagged and borne away.
Or myself, in nineteen forty-two.

The line dies, says the artist,
if it only outlines. Think of a line as an edge,
as the edge of a form
that is moving away from you in space.

And I do, as I trace your profile,
your edges, the slope of your shoulders
while you sit by the fire, curved to the book
you hold with both hands.

The Present

I guess it's not unexpected
that it's taken longer to stop
indulging the colorful flashbacks
—just like a movie
—almost as corny, with music
—with the trick of the blur, the swirl,

so driving past Naughties on Broad Street
I see him so clearly, I let the whole scene unspool:
he leaves here for some reason,
he leaves here for some reason, and returns.

His is the energy of happiness,
his smile and the sly/shy offering
of the penis-tipped lipstick—
it's his present for the day.
How could someone so present be so dead.

December 2001

In the hundred hues of sorrow
Tonight is the color of fog
No memory of your face
How could that be?
All day I've been sick to my stomach
I suspect the mail, so empty
Of you, so full of spores
I make another drink anyway

Were you once right here?
Why can't I picture you doing
That little tap-step by the stove.

The Glutton of Grief

Over the funeral meats
the glutton of grief
holds the oily chop
to the teeth, gobbles
the plump loin,
slurps the goblet
the left hand holds,
dribbles at the lips,
the eyes. Unseemly
gurgles, moans, no one
else at the table
could be so hungry, no
one else is even there
at the laden board.

Then they *are* there,
holding their polite plates.

Sweep it all into your mouth.
Let them starve.

Driving Alone

Months of miles down the mourning road
here's the stab of *left out.* The cut
in the heart that must first have been made
when eight girls in sixth grade
turned their backs on me
at a round table for eight.

Fifty years later I'm driving past
a circle of men in front of Dodd's Store
and I ache to know what they're saying—
the same with the couple in a truck I'm behind
who're taking the curves down the mountain
slow, leaning toward one another—
and later, the clutch of women in a church
parking lot who know some secret
that's making them laugh.
Then I get hurt by the birds on a wire,
their heads all bent in the same direction,
hurt that I don't know what kind they are
or where they are going or what they eat—
and I'm stung by my failure to identify
a single tree that I pass in its pale new leaf
except a dogwood in its wounded white.
And I actually start crying when I see ahead
a perfectly tilled red rectangle of garden
because I don't know how it was plowed
or who worked it. Or where he is now.

Watching the Weather Channel

Is it raining on you, Linda,
down in San Antonio—
raining too much?
Here in Virginia
the grass breaks
under our feet; the creek's
left stones for cows to lick.
The TV screen shows us cracks
in the earth where there used to be hay,
simulated systems massing
and fading over the globe.
We say we pray for rain
but what do we know
about asking for what we need?
We pray for the hurricane
to go around *you*—but send us its fringe,
the way we pray for the hand of Death
to pass on to another geography.

Cow Bone Clearing

From down in the hollow all afternoon
cows moan and bellow. How
could I know. On Long Mountain
I've heard their voices, the lowing,
the call and response of one cow
to another, a calf to a mother,
a mother to calf. But still from below
into the gold of the walnut's falling,
evening of first month of fall, still
the chorus of bellowing rises
like earth turning dark behind me
and now
in an hour before dawn I sit at the window
and look down the unceasing
sound in the dark and I know
the ache of a mother.
The loss like no other.
We allow even cows our pity for hours,
for the gorging milk, the unsuckled bloat,
the absence below,
in a meadow of shadows.

Not long ago I followed
a trail off the old Bough Road
down through thick laurel and cedar
and discovered a clearing where
flickers of sunlight fell on white bones—
cow skulls staring, a score of white skulls,
a row of curved ribs,
pearled pelvic rounds—
and though not a bird or a cricket called
it seemed that the sound I hear now from the hollow
rose from that bone ground, long and low.

Everybody's Coming in for the Winter

The slick-furred mouse scratches and scumbles
somewhere between the walls of my bedroom
and the sheathing of this old house. Between
the ceiling and shingles a squirrel gallops.
Damn them, noises in the dark, invisible squatters
it's taken me years to identify—
it's the groundhog under the flooring
who bumps and grinds to deepen his burrow.
But why so early, gnawing around in my inner mazes,
when summer's long season has not let go?
I'm listening, sleepless alone in our bed,
to the sounds of aliveness moving in:
How do they know
in the summery southern middle of night
that it's time to leave the kudzu caves,
the grassy banks, the fields and trees?
How do the creatures clambering around me
know it's time, know it's time, know it's time
to come in.

Redbud, Dogwood, and Crow

Jesus! If I saw a tree deep pink as dawn,
another white as a weightless cloud, I'd doubt
the first was called a Judas Tree, the other's
blossoms meant to depict the nailholes of Christ.
I would say nothing so cheerful, so vitally Spring,
could speak of betrayal, or bloom as suffering.
I'd call in that crow over there
to flap over to the redbud, then
fly up to a high dogwood branch,
and sit.
A big patch of black
crowing like a rowdy drunk
siphoning misnomers from innocence
and shouting them into the wind.

You, Archie Ammons

A. R. Ammons (1926–2001)

You're now a *curl of motion spent,*
edited into the anthologies, misunderstood
in the valleys and lichen-ledges

But much that you said
I took in, how to catch Spring
a second go-round by climbing

a mountain, how to write short
and live long, how to bray
shy as a trillium

and find eternity in a grain
of garbage, so much you
thought, you taught me to think

along with you, the improbability
of a caring cosmos, the notion of whether
we're cared for or not, we're in it for keeps.

How Space Travel Affects the Aging

1. What Their Bodies Know

They're not used to it.
There's a lot their bodies have learned
to endure,
though,
facing a mirror or fingers—
yours or someone else's—
where a part of you is missing
or added.
Gravity
too little, too much
floating, free falling, pinned to the Earth
in magnetic boots going nowhere.
Thus patience in one place—
a sightseer unable to hike mysterious
mountains seen from a window,
take the old bike up those blue curves
or swim for miles in a foreign sea.
Sight: eyes will not be portholes long.
Perspective:
how space travel affects the aging
is a question that makes them laugh.
They know where they're going next

2. Italics Mine

> Researchers hope the sleep experiment will help explain
> why so many astronauts sleep one to three hours less each
> night in orbit than they do on Earth, and *why the elderly
> tend to have trouble sleeping on Earth.*
>   —The Associated Press

trouble sleeping on Earth
trouble sleeping on Earth
troubled sleepers on Earth
Earth on sleeping trouble

one hundred, ninetyfive
ninety, eightyfive, eight-
-y, seventyfive, seventy.
sixtyfive, sixty, fiftyfive
trouble sleeping on Earth
Earth. Earth. Earth. Earth

earth hearth heart further
heart hurt hear ear earth
birth breathe eat beat be
trouble sleeping on
earth trouble sleeping
on earth trouble
sleeping on earth

3. John Glenn Hires Literary Agent

The Associated Press, November 3, 1998

But when he came down
he found he was wordless
having stored so few in his life

when it came down to
writing about it he found
he kept thinking of birds

how when they come down
from the air they're at home in
they perch on a branch and sing

4. How the Aging Affect Space Travel

No crew
No tests
Below
Just Blue
And you,
Weightless

Singapore Art Museum in the Rain

More than a century of sticky boys
and Christian Brothers sweating in long robes
raised their faces to the open arches
when a hot wind blew down the Straits
rattling the palm fronds that clicked
like marbles in a bag, or bamboo sticks played
down louvered shutters by students out
to make a clatter.

Now the boys and brothers gone,
the old verandas have been glazed
with ultraviolet-blocking windows
that in this gallery protect the replica
of Leonardo's flying man.

A guard barks twice, a black-eyed child
from Thailand withdraws his starfish hand
from an invention of the man of Vinci
who couldn't keep his hands off anything.

Suddenly outside the graygreen glass
the famous rain of Singapore
spills down the afternoon,
pours through glistening frets of palm leaves,
glazes the black taxies on Bras Basah Road.
And where the gutters meet the corners,
water arcs like fountains.

Inside, the priceless Leonardo painting
flown over the Red and Arabian seas,
the tip of India, the Bay of Bengal:
John the Baptist as a Youth,
a curly haired Italian with a secret smile,
a boy who could be gazing out the window
contemplating water.

The Last Paintings of Manet

Yesterday, Manet the painter suffered the amputation of a leg.
Gangrene had set in and reduced the flesh to such a degree
that the toenails came away upon contact.
—*Le Figaro*, April 1883

His last sixteen pictures are all
of flowers, small oils
of a few fresh stems
brought by friends to his bedside.

Most are in water, in one
of four glass vases
in his last room
or in his memory.

In the last painting of white lilacs,
in the flat-sided crystal vase,
the background is black.

The water and glass sparkle with white paint;
the edges of the lilac cones, massed and drooping,
are flecks of white paint. The white dazzles flatly
against the deep black ground.

It is no sunny day by a trellis in Givergny.
City man, city man, they say
he loved Monet, but not nature.
Flowers were on bars in the Folies Bergere.
Nature was not on the mind of the man at the picnic.

In the last paintings of Manet
the quick stems in water delight us—
lilacs, lilacs, green leaves and crystal—
though the light at the end of his brush is all there is.

Euripides' Cave

In Pericles' city, cold marble nights,
Protagoras, Socrates, pacing beside me,
ideas like stars arcing, or steadily blazing, or falling.
Mornings of papyri, mounting in rolls.
Reports of the War.

Afternoons, the agora, democracy's
broil. Men tricked out in the old dried skins
of politics, masculine voices
braying the many tongues of money,
reports from the War.
Believers bellowing gods like crowds at the races
urging their runner on with more noise.
So many signs to interpret—and I
with an eye for significance:
which citizen is rich, whose ignorance will kill
whose wife if back at home, unclasping
another man's warm gold necklace.

And all through the days of the sun,
the glare of the theater rising around me.
Tiers of men hoarding their careful prizes,
bearing down on my actors,
surrounding my circle of chosen words
with ceaseless mutter and drone.

There's a simple boat I can row
to Salamis.
In a cave I call mine
I fire my light.
In Salamis I wait for the women in silence.

Late sun falls on the stones of the entry
on the one sail in the dark blue Gulf.
It is so quiet, I hear Andromache crying,
Phaedra's whispers, Medea breathing
before the screams.

Stealing Grace

Suspicion was always sneaking—
from mountain thicket to woodpile
from an offshore boat to the beach—
so I entertained one for decades.

Suspicion was whispered
in services beyond my belief,
signaled in signs I was blind to.
Worse, shouted so loud I lowered my ears,
printed so boldly and badly I shuttered my eyes.

But suspicion still sneaked.
Something called grace was being delivered to people not me.
For one thing you had to believe in the sense of the word itself
and there was no way in the world it made sense to me
except that I couldn't dance.
Couldn't move in the arms of a man to a musical beat.
Couldn't smack ball against racket before it has passed.
Bumped into doors, wrote words from the left, in short
was gauche.

I decided to steal it.
And that's why you've caught me here
lurking in library stacks under *G*,
studying grace and how to grab it.
Excuse me, excuse me,
I was just leaving—

empty handed but hopeful,
off to the mountains where there have been moments,
there have been times in absolute solitude
when, for no discernible reason,
my body has stepped out and danced.

Blessing the Water Snakes

Unaware is the word that Coleridge used
and I'd try to explain to my sophomores
what I couldn't explain to myself.
But, yes, I see now, how it is
after the long sail down, the Doldrums, the deaths,
the hallucinatory orange sun. "Alone,
alone, all, all alone."
Who could believe in anything?
Who could believe in anything?
But the Mariner saw the water snakes
and blessed their beauty unaware.

An hour's drive up from sea level
there's a rise and a bend in the highway
where the Blue Ridge comes into view
like an ocean of gentle waves when
you're swimming among them, pushing
up with one foot against the squishy sand
to ride up over and down the swell
and I catch myself pushing the accelerator,
smiling unaware.

Today planting seeds, zinnia and cosmos,
the flakes from last winter's dead flowers
that can disappear from your hand if you don't
get them under the breeze and a few crumbs of earth,
my back was to the pathside wall of trumpet vine, raspberry,
honeysuckle, woven into the woof of locust trunks backed
by mountain's slope. When I turned
first I shivered, then I smiled. And then I smiled
at myself, eye level with a coppery snake.
Alone and smiling unaware.

Something gives way then, something heavy snaps
apart at my neck and slides weightily down my body.
and what have I done, not believing in anything,
to deserve this light air?

The Californian

Larry Levis, in memory

It was almost fall in the Blue Ridge
and among these small mountains
he seemed content to be so far east.

He leaned against the doorjamb
blending his cigarette smoke with afternoon haze
and asked after the apples
dense on my tall, unpruned tree.

An old vineyard hand,
he knew the uses of the earth's fruits.

They go unpicked, I said.
The deer get the lower ones,
the groundhogs the windfall.
September, the air smells like brandy.

You need a ladder, he said.

This other August, the thunder over,
the lightning and downpour over,
as I walk out to the rain-soaked tree,
a heavily laden branch near the top
cracks and softly thrashes down.

In the gust of the after-breeze
the wet apple leaves sprinkle my hair
as I bend to pick from the broken bough—
for there on the earth
are the perfect ripe apples, glistening and easy,
easier than anyone has a right to expect.

Black Animals

If it had been a dream
interpreters would've had a field day.

For out of the field, that day,
a black bull appeared in my fenced yard,
and halfway through my cabin's opened door
a black snake nosed the air.

And I was obligated to be
down in the valley by sunset
to honor my friend from England.
I was already late and had to leave
a snake that was either inside or out
(he'd disappeared when I turned for something to throw)
and a black bull who might later be parked on
the unlit path to my door.

Is this enough information?
Will you ask what happened next?
Or can you imagine the drive in the dark after dinner
back up the mountain
only knowing what was ahead
by each higher curve
as it came in my headlights.
Can you realize this is the end of my story, and yours?

NEW POEMS

The Owner Is Leaving This House

The owner is leaving this house
the slow way, giving it time
to get used to her absence.

She removes a painting, a table
(a small one), not so much
that the house would notice—

though the guest feels a draft
and notices a window uncovered.
A coffeepot's missing, the top

left library bookshelf is empty.
The bright rooms aren't dimmed,
really, but dusted, as the pollen outside

slightly powders late April—
drifts over wisteria
on its way out.

This house must be suspicious
at least of a season changing,
of something going on.

Here Comes Something and I Can't Lock the Door

Brand-new door has a screwed-up lock
and some kind of wind edging up a hurricane
is mashing against its double-paned glass
about to slap it like the scrapboard screendoor
it replaced.
The cat's dancing.
Fleetwood Mac after all these years.
Cat's snappy, I can't say I'm normal.
Something's coming and I'm alone
on a mountain.
Wind is tonight's owl
sounding like something to know.

Would Someone Want to Poison Me?

It seems so old-fashioned,
so Shakespearean. In Hamlet alone,
poison dispatches King, Queen, and Prince.

It seems so dated to poison a person.
Agatha Christie? P. D. James?
Yet recent events prove it's still going on.

Yushchenko was slipped his in a drink
but survived from black back to handsome.
His enemies we can surmise.

So who could be poisoning me?

Watching my skin bruise, my graying face,
the overall weakness of slumping muscles,
I consider my toxic unraveling,
my eventual unsolved painful demise.
The foreign hospital, the rustle and
whispers in no words I know—

Send the police, the CIA. Someone must pay
for doing me in.

Ten Days in France in April

You forget what people out of the country of cancer do,
the long mornings of idle talk over café au lait,
meandering plans for the afternoon's meanders,
a mossbanked stream branched with paths and footbridges—
death steps back, then out of the room, then out of the dooryard garden
beyond the new grass meadows and the brown plowed fields.
More light each day until by the end of the week
the air *IS* light. Even the late hour fall of darkness
is full of light, brushing on your face, starring the sky.
The laughter of friends on the path ahead
or heard from another room
so normal and present, so light and healthy,
so oblivious to anyone's ending.

The Irony of Poppies

Over their limber stems
the beautiful paper-thin
poppies let blood
light in, glow red
through a field the wind
the gentle wind
blows right and left
dealing death
and money, *Papaver*
nodding, somnolent,
gleaning a seed pod
pregnant with heroin.

A Poem Too Short for Its Subject

We brought the barricades into our bed,
the riots in the streets, the Rolling Stones,
my skirts up to my thighs. You were misled.
We brought the barricades into our bed.
You wanting me, me wanting action, poems instead
of swiping the Formica, ladies on the phone.
We brought the barricades into out bed,
like riots in the streets, like rolling stones.

ADD

Four plus twenty
equals blackbirds.
Mama baked a pie.
Are blackbirds crows
with better word?
Not so good in pie
that's open—
birds begin to sing.
Pi is taught here, only I
can spell Pythagoras
I've touched inside
a triangle
inside a circle too
one feels sharp
the other smooth
When the circle's open
the birds begin to sing.
A blackbird's in the parking lot
on Mr. Felton's car, Mr. Felton's
in it, kissing Mrs. Pharr.
A plus B is equal C,
long side sliding down.

Not So Bad as Labor Without an Epidural

My measurement is different from
the wounded Vietnam Vet's. He and I test
everything since the sixties to our sixties
by the yardstick of our worst pain.

I guess it's good to learn at twenty-four
or younger what it's like to hope to die.
"You won't remember," said my doctor,
who himself remembers nothing now.

So the Vet and I can get the gout, cracked
ribs, bad knees, arthritis, migraines,
but still we say it's not so bad as that.
And as for deeps of sadness settling in

I remember Bonnie's boyfriend,
just back from Vietnam, bragged
of bayoneting gooks in hootches.
His eyes were tanked with sadness.

I left the room and went upstairs
and vomited, because I was pregnant.

Widow's Walk

Do you believe that friends you walk
with now think you're okay?
Maybe some do. But some don't.
You and I are walking the footbridge
high over the white water river
that splits Richmond's city,
a bridge suspended from the highway
above us that thumps with traffic.

Winds blowing down the James
carry off our careful conversation.
We bump into each other avoiding
cyclists, then hold on to the railing
looking down into whipped-up rapids
where the kayaker died last month
the same day Richard did.

It's a warm day in February,
even with the winds, more like May.
I love it.

But I know what you're thinking
as we let go the rail:
Why I am up here on this bridge?
Why is it swaying? Why are the rapids
swirling, the friend beside me crazy?

What pounding noise around us?
Why did I just use the phrase
"Aside from my sorrow . . ."?

Creation Theory

Their necks and shoulders slumped.
The perfect flowers drooped the same,
all the birds were crestfallen.

They were watched as they walked out
and so were the vine stems unwinding,
the leaves on the beanpoles withering.

The adamant seeds of bindweed, kudzu,
Ironwood, and thistle put down roots
as it had long been known they would.

Their suckers smothered the meadowgrass,
blocked the sun from the pomegranate tree.
Thorns were born, for their own reasons.

Vigil

There were lies
at the dying.
No amens
from me.

But I honor
my liars
who spoke only words
emptied of everything
except truth.

The Tiny Fig Wasp It Cannot Live Without

And that's just one type, a fig tree
in Africa. What about our apple
trees blossoming with no buzz.
All that pink scent
sent out unanswered,
we'll be appleless in August.
Oh, symbiosis.
What we don't know
that we cannot live without.
What we didn't know growing
up, stepping on spiders,
squishing ants. We sprayed
DDT at wasps, at bees,
whatever stung us.
Quick Henry the Flit.
Do you remember it? How it
cracked the fragile shells?
We didn't notice the leaking yolks
until there were no eagles.

February Burglary

Winter's erasure outside

stem and leaf and petal missing

Inside the old house
spaces are full of space

colder than the weather

The Sheriff takes pictures of absence
says it's going on
up here, furniture . . .

The old log walls
are accustomed to change

strangers

The windows watch
for different arrangements
inside and out

August Evening

Silence rises
from the lower meadow

the bowed wet grasses
struck dumb by storm

but it can't hush
the monotonous drop

of the dripping gutter
on the metal shovel

Still

silence tries
in this twilight

to insinuate itself
like steam from the wet deck

before rising up through cicadas
up over the crickets, the owls

to fall in the small hours.

Dumb Bunny

I'm looking right at it; this rabbit
is eating grass or clover three feet from me
beside the edge of my garden and won't be
frightened away. My dog if I had one
would gobble her up in a minute
so I bark but she just sits chewing.
The fur on the curve of her spine
is curling backward in the humid air.
I remember the shock when I saw
the paperback cover of my first book curling
up on a table in Chapel Hill.
I knew a lot about southern summers
but not that my long dreamed-of cover would
roll itself back on my name.
Dumb bunny's still there, and me, barking.

Weather Reporters

What can men with microphones
in whipping ponchos tell you,
wind howling on their words?

The palm trees bend behind their backs.
But as long as his wiring is working,
how can we worry about Mike Seidel?

The last wet reporter flung out
of the picture would cause us alarm.
Click and black.

When no one can report the trouble
we're in, we'll head for the basement
or attic, or ditch, depending on conditions.

September 2011

It keeps on happening again and it will
be forgotten again until it's September.
We're in the tall building paying the bill

overdue to the city for gas to fuel
our furnace. We're thinking *November*—
it keeps on happening again—and we'll

need heat. Now it's still summer, too hot until
fall to turn off the AC. Consider
that other cloudless day, paying the bill

in City Hall. It's way too high now, still
we pay it. Look at the line, at him, her—
it keeps on happening again and it will.

Energy's costly. We forget it can kill.
Though some of our children can't remember,
we in the building paying the bill

look at the date, at the window sill,
think of the choice between jump and tinder.
It keeps on happening again and it will.
We're in the tall building, paying the bill.

The Brain's Refusal

I will not serve,
says the brain.

The mind sits smugly behind it
agreeing: "I prefer not to."

The sound body stumbles.
Insurgents wither the strongholds.

The brain refuses, digs in.
Opponents are diffused.

From its trenches, memory
persists, but ducks and covers.

From its hilltop, the General
of synapse retreats

crosses over the North River
to lie down under the shade of the trees.

Woman Drowning in Her House

Sculptor Myron Helfgott has sewn together Mylar to
fashion a house, inserting a photograph of a woman
before he stitches the roof top. The work is untitled.

Why is there no protest,
no twisted features
mashed against the glass
like a woman
in a car gone off
a bridge, sinking fast?

Her smiling face
in this sealed Mylar house
is like the happy frog
warm before the boil.
Or the woman who left
on the spigots for years
and got used to the noise.

A Version Of

My life has been
a version of being
as has yours and Barry's dog life
(privileged but with hard losses).
The bird who hit my plate glass
but never went hungry in this seedberry acre
or thirsty living near a creek
was a version of a bird's life.
Isn't it something to think of?
How unique we are not just in feature but in span
not just in luck but in plate glass
and that doesn't begin to account for
the climate, vicinity, or hunger
of your version.

Sacrificial Metal

Soldiers rolled
in the last wave
scalloping the sand
until their whole bodies
were metallic with wet grit.

Eight or ten, the men moved
from one side to the other
in unison. They seemed to know
what they were doing.
Men in civvies stood over them.

At Virginia Beach four
old ladies pushed themselves up
from lowslung beach chairs,
walked slowly toward Fort Story,
saw dolphins in the ocean, soldiers rolling.

Philip Larkin on Hearing a Poem

Larkin said that hearing a poem
as opposed to reading it
means you miss so much—
the shape, punctuation, italics,
"knowing how far you are from the end."

Yes. Hear a poem, you never know.
Is the poem quoting another poet?
Was that line ironically italicized?

Where are the breaks?

One poem's painful, drawn-out ending
is like not knowing how far you are.

The voice drones, each page flipped
like a tedious day of the long haul, chronic
continuousness, no news from the doctors.

Listeners shift in their seats
like caregivers aching from constancy.
Even the poet seems uncertain
how far she is from the end.

Rounding the Curve by the Fake Police Car

Alligators laughed after
a while, or looked to us like laughing—
flattened, strapped to the truck backs.
Carriers of alligators, movers of
Lauderdale, we loaded 'em up
for an Everglade dump.

We showed our grandkids
this one old swamp raised and paved,
drove past an empty gatehouse, each piece
of yard, its touch of jungle.
Round the curve, the fake police car
by the docks of yachts.

Christmas Eve, You in Florida

Paintings play tricks like this one
across from my bed at midnight.
Tomorrow two figures will be
standing there on a beach.

Now, the ocean is only a curve,
the sand a kind of white, a white
only white because the rest is ocean
in shades of dark blue.

Tonight, you can hear the ocean
from your curve out of its sight.
You could go walk the dark beach
and be a figure no one can see.

You could listen to waves be
hymns in the midnight choir
in The Church By the Sea
down your street.

Poems change colors too,
some times not a soul is there.
Or maybe in a poem, morning light
will show two people on a beach.

Skating up to Eighty

As if we could glide, swoop on the ice
this way and that, as if we were lithe
and perfectly balanced.

As if we could do a duet, a pas de deux,
but I never could follow you
or match your feet to Marvin Gaye.
As if we could even fox-trot! Or waltz,
or promenade at the Saint Cecelia.

As if we'd ever walked a line

Or marched in time,
or marched in time.

Florida

Planting a plumbago in the rain,
a warm rain, he keeps going,
digging a difficult hole
with old hands, old tools—
a rusty axe to slice
the roots of palm and tough
clumped fern, a mattock to free
enough of earth.
He lifts the wet plant gently
and pats it in, blooming blue,
then heads for the shed
with the tools in the rain.

The Span

From the old bridge we'd been stopped on,
a little below us, it looked like a diving board.
When the girl switched her sign from *Stop* to *Slow*
I saw across the river three men standing like old-
fashioned divers at its base, newsreels we'd seen
of men in swimcaps. "Hard hats," you literal you.

You agreed with "like a diving board," but no spring
to it. Something below was holding it up, something
concrete. It was the business of your life. Concrete—
but for me the men were waiting their turn over there,
each to compete for the best two-and-a-half gainer
to knife the Tye River. They'd die, you said.

"That's a fine span," I learned, "a very long one—
they didn't make 'em like that back then." Or us
either, I thought as I almost saw the Hard Hat bounce
at the tip, his one knee up to his waist.
"Inspectors," you said as we drove alongside, "lolly-
gagging." Whichever. Our span is ready.

CPSIA information can be obtained at www.ICGtesting.com
Printed in the USA
BVOW07s1227050814

361434BV00004B/25/P